I DRIVE AN AMBULANCE

by **Sarah Bridges**

illustrated by **Derrick Alderman** & **Denise Shea**

PICTURE WINDOW BOOKS
Minneapolis, Minnesota

Thanks to our advisers for their expertise, research, and advice:

Robert Ball, Paramedic
Hennepin County Medical Center
Minneapolis, Minnesota

Pamela M. Roquemore, NREMT
Harvey, Louisiana

Susan Kesselring, M.A., Literacy Educator
Rosemount-Apple Valley-Eagan
(Minnesota) School District

John L. Roquemore
President, National Association of EMTs,
Jefferson, Louisiana

Managing Editors: Bob Temple, Catherine Neitge
Creative Director: Terri Foley
Editors: Brenda Haugen, Christianne Jones
Editorial Adviser: Andrea Cascardi
Designer: Nathan Gassman
Storyboard development: Amy Bailey Muehlenhardt
Page production: Banta Digital Group
The illustrations in this book were rendered digitally.

Picture Window Books
151 Good Counsel Drive
P.O. Box 669
Mankato, MN 56002-0669
877-845-8392
www.capstonepub.com

All books published by Picture Window Books
are manufactured with paper containing at least
10 percent post-consumer waste.

Library of Congress Cataloging-in-Publication Data
Bridges, Sarah.
I drive an ambulance / by Sarah Bridges ; illustrated by
   Derrick Alderman and Denise Shea.
p. cm. — (Working wheels)
Includes bibliographical references and index.
ISBN-13: 978-1-4048-0618-4 (hardcover)
ISBN-10: 1-4048-0618-0 (hardcover)
ISBN-13: 978-1-4048-1862-0 (paperback)
ISBN-10: 1-4048-1862-6 (paperback)
1. Emergency medical technicians—Juvenile literature.
   2. Ambulance drivers—Juvenile literature. I. Alderman,
   Derrick. II. Shea, Denise. III. Title. IV. Series.
RC86.5.B75 2004
362.18'8—dc22   2003028231

Printed in the United States of America in North Mankato, Minnesota.
092010   005956R

My name is Nina, and I drive an ambulance. My partner and I help people who are hurt or sick.

HOSPITAL

An emergency medical technician, or EMT, and a paramedic work as partners in the ambulance. While the EMT drives, the paramedic rides in the back next to the patient.

My ambulance looks like a big, **boxy** truck. The front of the ambulance has a driver's seat and a passenger's seat.

The word AMBULANCE appears backward on the front of the vehicle. When other drivers look in their rear-view mirrors, the word appears the right way.

The paramedic sits on a long bench in the back of the ambulance. Beside the bench is space for a stretcher.

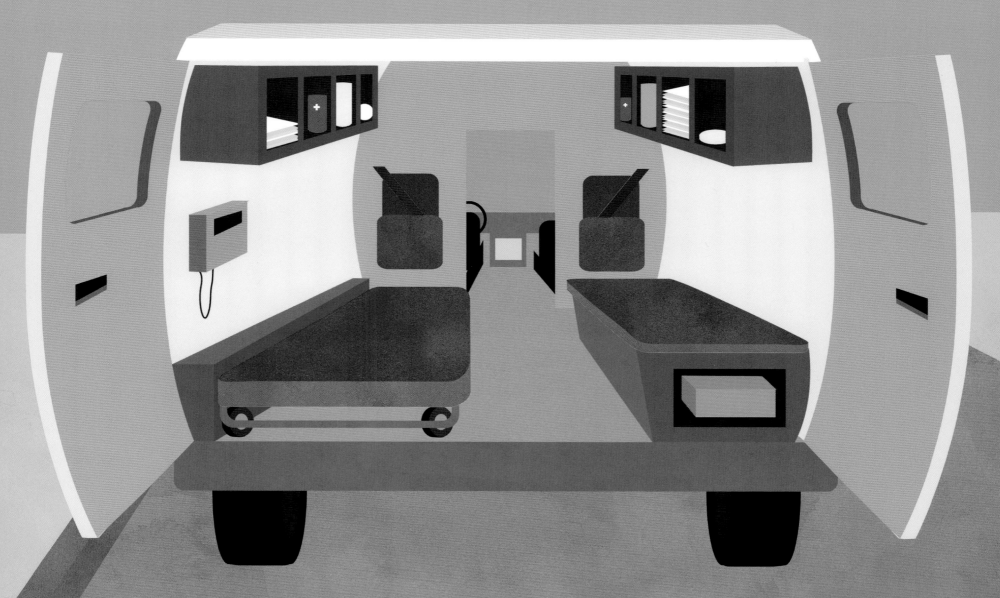

Here comes a call from the dispatcher. A patient needs our help. I switch on the flashing lights and siren. This lets people know they must move out of the way.

The wail of the siren is so **LOUD**,
it is hard to hear anything else!

The law says that other drivers must pull over to the side of the road to let an ambulance pass.

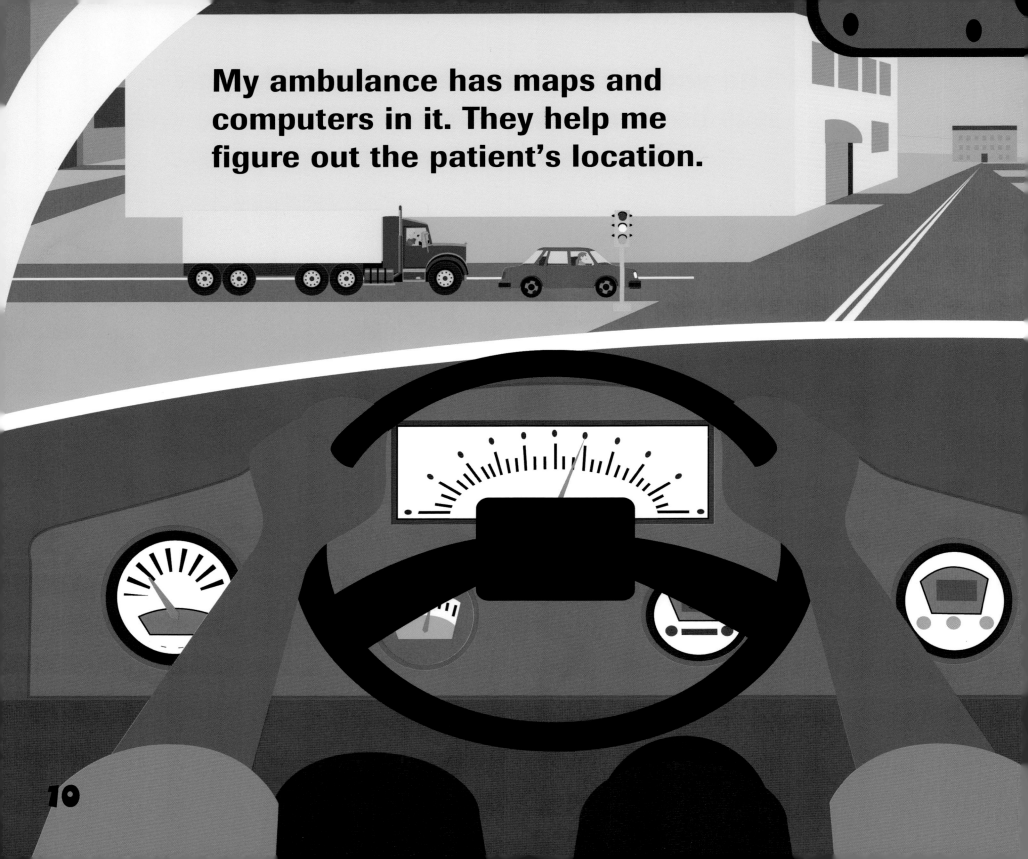

My ambulance has maps and computers in it. They help me figure out the patient's location.

10

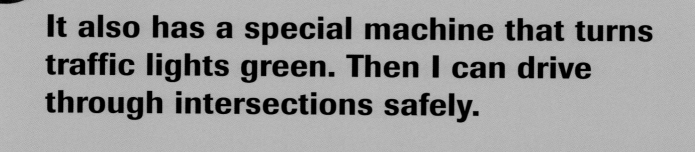

It also has a special machine that turns traffic lights green. Then I can drive through intersections safely.

Newer ambulances have GPS (global positioning system) receivers that tell ambulance drivers how to find an address.

When we get to the patient, my partner tries to find out what is wrong. She listens to the person's lungs with a stethoscope. She checks his pulse and blood pressure.

I bring in the stretcher from the ambulance. The ambulance carries a lot of medical equipment for us to use.

The most common problems that EMTs and paramedics find are heart and breathing problems.

In most cases, I use my radio to call a doctor at the hospital. The doctor tells me how I should help the patient.

My partner and I strap the patient on a stretcher. We carry him to the ambulance.

Paramedics are allowed to give people certain medicines without talking to a doctor.

The ambulance races to the hospital. The siren **blares**, and the lights **flash**. Doctors and nurses meet us when we get to the emergency room.

At the hospital, doctors and nurses continue to care for the patient. The paramedic tells the doctors what happened to the patient as they drove to the hospital.

17

Even though the patient is at the hospital, my job is not done. I must clean the ambulance between calls. I use special chemicals to kill germs.

Then I refill my supplies and get ready for the next call from the dispatcher.

Ambulances are like small hospitals on wheels. Just like hospitals, ambulances need to be kept very clean.

19

When my workday is done, my ambulance will be used by the next EMT and paramedic team.

After the new team does a safety check, the ambulance is off on another trip.

Safety is very important. Every two weeks, a mechanic checks the ambulance's brakes, engine, and tires.

AMBULANCE DIAGRAM

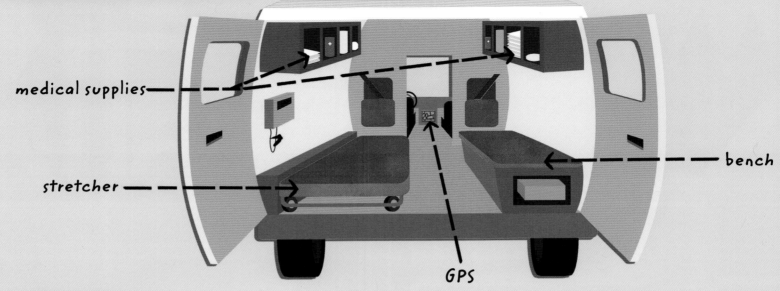

medical supplies

stretcher

bench

GPS

GLOSSARY

dispatcher—the person who answers calls to 911 and tells the ambulance where to go

emergency medical technician (EMT)— a person who is trained and allowed to treat patients and drive an ambulance

global positioning system (GPS)—a computer that receives signals from satellites in the sky

paramedic—a person who treats patients before they reach the hospital and also can drive an ambulance; a paramedic has more training in patient care than an EMT does

stethoscope—a tool used to listen to a person's heart and lungs

stretcher—a bed with straps and wheels that paramedics use to move patients

FUN FACTS

 Before cars were invented, horses pulled ambulance carts to the hospital. The carts were open, and the ride was bumpy. Sometimes rain fell on patients!

 Some of the first ambulances that had motors looked like station wagons. It was impossible to stand up in one.

 Doctors used to ride in the back of ambulances to care for sick people. In the 1960s, paramedics replaced most doctors in ambulances. Doctors rarely ride in ambulances anymore.

 Paramedics have a special kind of wheelchair that lets them carry patients down narrow stairways. This special wheelchair is called a stair chair.

 As they speed along, ambulance drivers need to watch carefully for other cars. Many people hear the sirens and move in front of ambulances by mistake.

HOSPITAL

TO LEARN MORE

At the Library

Bingham, Caroline. *Big Book of Rescue Vehicles*. New York: Dorling Kindersley, 2000.

Ethan, Eric. *Ambulances*. Milwaukee. Gareth Stevens, 2002.

Hanson, Anne E. *Ambulances*. Mankato, Minn.: Bridgestone Books, 2001.

Teitelbaum, Michael. *If I Could Drive an Ambulance*. New York: Scholastic, 2003.

On the Web

FactHound offers a safe, fun way to find Web sites related to this book. All of the sites on FactHound have been researched by our staff. www.facthound.com

1. Visit the FactHound home page.

2. Enter a search word related to this book, or type in this special code: 1404806180.

3. Click on the FETCH IT button.

Your trusty FactHound will fetch the best Web sites for you!

INDEX

BOOKS IN THIS SERIES

- I Drive an Ambulance
- I Drive a Bulldozer
- I Drive a Dump Truck
- I Drive a Garbage Truck
- I Drive a Semitruck
- I Drive a Snowplow